POP PEOPLE™
Backstreet Boys!

By Devra Newberger Speregen

Scholastic Inc.
New York Toronto London Auckland Sydney
Mexico City New Delhi Hong Kong

This book is unauthorized and is not sponsored by the Backstreet Boys, their representatives, or anyone involved with them.

Photo credits
Front cover: B. Khan/Retna; Page1: Mark Cairns/Retna; Page 2: Amary/ Shooting Star; Page 3: John Gladwin/Retna; Page 4: Doug Peters/Retna; Page 5: Larry Busacca/Retna; Page 6: Wilberto Boogaard/Retna; Page 7: Larry Miller/Retna; Page 8 & 9: Clavel/Shooting Star; Page 10: Larry Busacca/ Retna; Page 11: Melanie Edwards/Retna; Page 12: Henry Lamb/Ron Galella Ltd; Page 13: Melanie Edwards/Retna; Page 14: (top) Bob Berg/Retna; Page 14: (bottom) Kari Sellards/Shooting Star; Page 15: Kelly Swift/Retna; Page 16: Steve Granitz/Retna

ISBN 0-439-22226-5

12 11 10 9 8 7 6 5 4   0 1 2 3 4 5/0

Printed in the U.S.A.
First Scholastic Printing, September 2000

CONTENTS

●

INTRODUCTION

•

Where will *you* be on October 7?

If you're a true Backstreet Boys fan, it doesn't matter *where* you'll be . . . as long as you'll be celebrating Backstreet Boys Day in America — an official holiday declared by Mayor Glenda Hood of Orlando, Florida! And if you're a true fan, you know Orlando, Florida, is the place where it all began for the five megatalented cuties, Nick Carter, Howie Dorough, Brian Littrell, A. J. McLean, and Kevin Richardson!

So, in honor of this truly special occasion, gather your buds, slip your BSB CDs (including the brand-new one) CAREFULLY from their cases, hang up even more glossy posters of the Boys, crack open this very cool book, and have yourself a BSB Bonanza Celebration!

10 WAYS TO CELEBRATE

1. Put on your own Backstreet performance to *Larger Than Life*. We *know* you know all the moves from the kickin' video — but please don't swing from the ceiling!
2. Put your BSB knowledge to the test and turn to page TK to take the BSB Trivia Challenge!
3. Swap stories with friends of your most perfect day hanging with the Backstreet Boys.
4. Play the BSB's newest CD over and over until you've memorized every song!
5. Create an artistic collage on oak tag or poster paper honoring the Boys . . . and mail it to them.
6. Write, star in, and film your own BSB video!
7. Decorate your bedroom walls with a montage of BSB posters and pix.
8. Host a BSB craft night with your friends. Make a keepsake box to store all of your BSB treasures — like concert ticket stubs and pins. Just cut out your favorite BSB pictures from magazines and newspapers, and glue them to the outside of a shoebox. Decorate with sequins, glitter, or buttons. It's that easy!

9. Whip up some great party food. Include the Boys' favorites: macaroni and cheese (Brian), Chinese (Howie), fried chicken (Kevin), chili cheese fries (A. J.), and wash it all down with Mountain Dew soda (Nick's favorite beverage)!

10. Play BSB-themed party games, like Pin the Grammy on a Backstreet Boy! Or play matchmaker and decide which Backstreet Boy is the perfect match for you and your friends.

CHAPTER 1

●

THE PHENOMENON

You can't go anywhere these days without encountering something Backstreet Boys–related. (And anyway . . . who would want to?) But no one's complaining, that's for sure. It's way cool getting a Backstreet BLAST at every turn during the day — hearing their newest hits on the radio, watching their freshest videos on MTV's *Total Request Live,* and laying eyes on their gorgeous faces plastered on magazine covers and Burger King posters!

If the boys were worried about the future of their careers seven years ago, they can certainly put all those fears to rest now. The Backstreet Boys have taken America — and the *world* — by storm, and they show *no* signs of letting up!

In the past year alone, the Backstreet Boys have:

- made more money than any other musician or band in the world — more than $187 million worldwide!
- sold out their 53-venue, three-month Millennium tour in ONE DAY!
- hit gold and platinum sales for their records in 45 countries!
- been immortalized in the Backstreet Project, a series of comic books from BSB Nick and Marvel Comic's top creator, Stan Lee.
- won such accolades as *People Magazine*'s Men We Love and The 25 Most Intriguing People, *Entertainment Weekly*'s Best Entertainers of the Year, and made the cover of *Rolling Stone* twice: May 27, 1999, and January 20, 2000.

And though they've never won a Grammy award (Unfair! Unfair!), they've snagged just about every other top music award, including American Music awards, *Billboard* awards, JUNO awards, MTV awards, and Nickelodeon Kids' Choice awards.

But wait . . . there's more!

Their recent on-line pay-per-view event, which ran from March through July 2000, was a tremendous success! By just logging on to the Web, BSB fans could watch an entire BSB concert and in-depth interviews with each of the Boys — or just watch the Boys play golf and hang out. Their third CD is generating masses of new fans before it even makes its debut, and the Boys *promise* their upcoming tour will be slammin'.

No doubt about it — they're successful. . . .

They're famous. . . .

And best of all, they're still the same five sweet guys they were back at the beginning of their careers.

So, how has such fame and fortune affected Nick Carter, Howie Dorough, Brian Littrell, A. J. McLean, and Kevin Richardson?

It's said in show business that you know you've made it when others start making fun of you. That was certainly true in the case of the Backstreet Boys a few short months ago. Just when the guys couldn't get any hotter, along came a new all-boy band called 2Ge+her — five hunky singers almost identical in look and sound to Nick, Howie, Brian, A. J., and Kevin.

Almost.

Because even though MTV's spoof creation 2Ge+her is jam-packed with cuties, not one of them holds a candle to any of the dreamy Backstreet Boys! 2Ge+her was formed by MTV as a *parody* of all-boy bands — to make fun of all the boy bands currently topping the pop charts. But, *duh*. With a futuristic CD cover shot, complete with an almost identical BSB pose, we know which all-boy band 2Ge+her is *really* poking fun at.

So are our Boys upset over any of this?

Not a chance!

In fact, Nick, Howie, Brian, A. J., and Kevin think 2Ge+her is a total goof! They get the joke and they don't feel threatened by Q. T., Jerry, Chad, Doug, and Mickey. The Backstreet Boys know what they have is *real*. Real songs, real videos . . . real *fans*.

"I think it's kind of flattering," Kevin told *CD-NOW* about 2Ge+her and all the other boy bands that have cropped up since BSB broke. "As long as everybody's making good music, it's all good."

"It *is* kind of flattering when people want to poke fun at you," Howie also admitted backstage at the JUNO Awards in March 2000.

And then there's O-Town.

O-Town is yet *another* all-boy band created in the image of the Backstreet Boys. Unless you've been living in a cave for the past few months, you know all about O-Town — the hot new boy band from ABC-TV's *Making the Band*. This show has been called a cross between MTV's *Real World* and the Backstreet Boys. In fact, one of the show's advisers is none other than Lou Pearlman —

the same music mogul who helped put the Backstreet Boys together.

O-Town (named for Orlando, the city in Florida where bands like BSB and 'N Sync were formed) may be topping the charts these days, but they're not a real concern for the Boys. Like Kevin said, there's enough room in the world for everybody! Plus, Kevin knows that what he and the other Boys have is special: a history. The guys worked long and hard to bring BSB to where they are today. They've stuck by one another through the best of times and the worst of times. That fact has brought them closer together than 2Ge+her could ever get!

So, spoof all you want, MTV! Keep bringing on the competition, ABC! Here in the real world, with a new CD, a new tour on the way, and a fresh, hot look, the Backstreet Boys are far from worried.

Unless, of course, 2Ge+her or O-Town think *they* have the power to sell 80,000 tickets in 73 minutes!

CHAPTER 2

IN THE BEGINNING . . .

By now, everyone's heard the story of how the Backstreet Boys got together. In 1993, A. J. McLean and Howie Dorough were introduced by their vocal coach in Orlando, Florida, and hit the auditioning circuit together. That's where they met Nick Carter. The trio sang a cappella at various auditions and decided to form a band. Then, one day at Disney World, they heard Kevin Richardson perform and were so impressed they asked him to join their trio. Together, the fab foursome beat out 50 other contenders at an Orlando audition held by manager Lou Pearlman for an all-boy band!

At that point, the guys all agreed they needed a fifth band member to round out their sound. Kevin suggested his cousin, Brian Littrell, and after a quick, convincing phone call, Brian was on a plane for Orlando.

Taking their name from a popular teen hangout in Orlando — the Backstreet Market on International Drive — the boys started touring in Europe and became a big hit in Germany. Then, after some very successful concert tours and record sales in Europe, the Boys hit Canada by storm. They returned to the United States in 1997.

It's been a long, hard road for the Backstreet Boys — in fact, American teens were not so ready to embrace them when they first returned. They were dismissed for a long time as just another all-boy pop band. But with the release of "Everybody (Backstreet's Back)" and "Quit Playing Games with My Heart," everything changed.

Those two tracks from their first album, *Backstreet Boys,* quickly became hits, capturing the hearts of pop-music fans all over the country. Before long, the Backstreet Boys phenomenon began to grow. In May 1999 they released their second album, *Millennium,* which sold 1.13 million copies in *one week* after its release. It broke Garth Brooks's record of 1.09 million sales in seven weeks and put the Backstreet Boys on top of the charts for months on end! The Boys sealed their fate by rockin' into the new millennium with a kickin'

North American tour appropriately titled Into the Millennium. The entire tour — 53 venues and 765,000 seats — sold out in about an hour. The Boys embarked on a touring experience that would make even the Beatles jealous.

And now they're ready to do it all over again. They've reinvented themselves — while promising not to change *too* much — and are proud to present the Backstreet Boys *after* the Millennium tour.

Millions of fans couldn't be happier!

The album displays each Boy's strength. "We feel like we've grown [on the new record]," Kevin told *CD-NOW*. "It's deeper lyrically, but it's not over our young fans' heads. We're just trying to keep with the times in order to stay in the pop-music scene . . . just like Madonna did, just like Janet and Michael [Jackson] did, so we'll have a long career."

According to Brian, if you don't change, your act gets *old*. So when the Boys went into seclusion this past summer to write new songs and reinvent themselves for this new album and tour, they ended up with something they're all very proud of. "We don't want to give everything away as of yet," Brian told MTV's John Norris, "but we've got a lot of new ideas in introducing the new album. . . . We want to show people that we can do!"

"That's how you stay on top," Nick added in the same MTV interview. "You've got to just keep recreating while the people are growing with you. Something new and something that's catchy to their ears that they're going to enjoy listening to."

No problem, guys — we'd love to see what fresh, new stuff the BSB have to offer! Just *please* — don't change *too* much!

CHAPTER 3

BACKSTREET BOYS: A TIME LINE

1993 — Lou Pearlman holds an open audition for an all-boy band in Orlando, Florida. Kevin, A. J., and Howie are chosen from thousands.

1993 — On April 19, Brian Littrell receives a call from his cousin Kevin to come audition. The next day Brian is on a plane to Orlando.

1993–1995 — The Backstreet Boys play at theme parks, junior high schools, and high schools. They win over many fans by singing great a cappella covers of their favorite Boyz II Men and Color Me Badd songs.

1994 — Their manager, Donna Wright, has the Boys perform for an executive at Jive Records. Jive signs the Backstreet Boys.

1995 — Their first single, "We've Got It Goin' On," is released in the U.S. and doesn't make it higher than 65 on Billboard's Top 100. But in Germany, where the single was released earlier, it tops the charts. The Boys tour Europe in 1995 and 1996.

1996 — Their first album, *Backstreet Boys,* is released in April, sells more than 11 million copies, and is certified platinum in 26 countries. The Backstreet Boys are a smash in Germany and in Canada.

1997 — The Boys tour the U.S. and release their album in the U.S. in August. Jive promotes their album heavily, giving free BSB cassettes with J. C. Penney makeup at cheerleader camps, and with books in the teen romance series *Love Stories*. The result? "Quit Playing Games with My Heart" and "As Long As You Love Me" hit the airwaves and never leave. Finally, the Backstreet Boys are a huge hit in the United States!

1998 — In May, Brian undergoes heart surgery to repair a heart murmur — a hole in his heart. More sadness when Howie's sister, Caroline, dies from lupus, and Brian's and Kevin's grandfather passes away.

1999 — In May, *Millennium* is released. One by one, the album's singles become number-one hits: "Larger Than Life," "I Want It That Way," "Show Me the Meaning of Being Lonely," and "The One." In October, Mayor Glenda Hood of Orlando declares October 7

Backstreet Boys Day in America. In November, the Boys embark on their Into the Millennium tour. The Boys win countless awards, including *Billboard* Music awards, Smash Hits awards, and World Music awards.

    2000 — The Boys tour until March. In April, they hit the studio again to write and record their newest album, which will tentatively be released on October 10, 2000. Burger King promotes their tour and offers free Backstreet CDs and videos at their restaurants.

CHAPTER 4

SAY IT AIN'T SO!

Unfortunately (for their fans at least), the rumors that flooded computer and telephone lines across the country a while back all proved to be true: Our beloved BSB cousins, Brian and Kevin, have both gotten down on their knees and proposed marriage to their sweeties — big fat diamond rings and all!

Many critics predicted that this news would devastate their fans. Many said it was the end for the Backstreet Boys — that BSB fans could never accept their idols marrying anyone else.

But those who could ever think a BSB fan would just STOP adoring one of the guys — for ANY reason — don't really understand what being a BSB fan is all about!

For one thing, BSB fans really *care* about the

Boys. So much so that they only want what's best for the guys — even if it means giving up their own dreams of ever being the one and only in their fave Boy's life. For this reason, BSB fans were happy for both Brian and Kevin when word broke of their engagements.

And why shouldn't they be?

There are still PLENTY OF SINGLE BACKSTREET BOYS LEFT!

The Love Stories

Kevin — old-fashioned romantic that he is — didn't dare pop the question to his lady, Kristin Willits, until he had spoken to her father. So last November during the Into the Millennium tour he took Kristin's father aside.

"He asked my permission to ask Kristin to marry him," John Willits (Kristin's father) told *People* magazine. "I told him I'd be honored."

At the time, Kristin was working in Europe (she was a dancer with Cher's concert tour). But when she returned to the U.S. right before Christmas, Kevin whisked her away on vacation to the Florida bed-and-breakfast where he'd first told her he loved her — and popped the question! According to some sources, he gave her a ring the following Valentine's Day.

Kevin's romantic proposal was very inspirational for his cousin Brian. Once Brian learned his cousin was getting married, he proposed to his girlfriend of three years, Leighanne Wallace — on Christmas night! He presented her with a four-karat canary yellow diamond and sapphire engagement ring.

"It was really sweet," Leighanne told *People* magazine. "I have this peace about me now."

"There's a right time for everything," Brian told *People*. "It's kind of like the jump start on getting on with life, so I'm looking forward to it."

The Lucky Girls

Kristin Willits is 29 and from Oklahoma. She works as a dancer; most recently she was on tour with Cher. Kristin has also danced with the famous Rockettes at Radio City Music Hall in New York City and played the part of a dancer in the Jim Carrey movie, *Man on the Moon*.

Kevin met Kristin in 1993 when she was dancing in *Beauty and the Beast* at Disney World and he was Leonardo, the Teenage Mutant Ninja Turtle. Kevin first noticed her in the employee cafeteria. "She walked into the cafeteria," he told *People,* "and it was like someone turned a light on."

The couple started dating, then Kevin joined the Backstreet Boys. His commitment to the band took him on the road a lot and dating proved to be difficult. "It's real, real hard," Kevin said a while back. "We've broken up quite often because of the traveling."

Leighanne Wallace is 30 years old, and some say she looks a lot like Britney Spears. She is an actress from Atlanta, Georgia, and has appeared in the movie *Wild America*, the TV show *Silk Stalkings,* and in a TV commercial with Jerry Seinfeld. She also appeared in the BSB videos *As Long As You Love Me* and *I'll Never Break Your Heart.* In fact, Leighanne met Brian in June 1997 when she was an extra on the set of *As Long As You Love Me.* Leighanne says that when she was sent to appear in the video, she had no idea who the Backstreet Boys were! Brian asked her out for Italian food the next night, and the two have been together ever since.

Brian knew he had a gem on his hands when Leighanne stuck by him in May 1998 after his heart surgery. "I didn't leave him until I knew he was in perfect health," she told *Star Magazine Online*. "It was one of the scariest times of my life."

Though they tried desperately to keep their wedding date a secret, the word leaked out that they were to be married on September 2, 2000, in Atlanta.

What about A. J., Nick, and Howie?

Don't worry, girls, there are still plenty of *single* BSB cuties. Although he didn't make a formal announcement at the time that Brian and Kevin did, A. J. may be the third BSB to pop the question. At least that's what was reported in a New York newspaper. A. J. and girlfriend Amanda Latrona may be planning a trip down the aisle in the not-so-distant future. But it doesn't look like Nick and Howie are getting married anytime soon. Although A. J., Brian, and Kevin have managed to meet the girls of their dreams, the Boys' busy schedules make serious relationships a challenge. And if Nick and Howie are dating anyone, they've chosen to keep their private lives private.

Although Howie *doesn't* see marriage in his immediate future, he admitted in a recent radio interview that he would eventually like to get married. "Maybe have a family, you know, have a couple of little Backstreet kids running around!"

As for Nick, when he was asked on the TV show, *Open House Party* if he was close to marriage his answer was "No, no, no, no!"

If I could marry one of the Backstreet Boys, it would be: _____

20

We would get married in: _____

_____.

My bridesmaids would be: _____

_____.

The best man and ushers would be: _____

_____.

Our wedding song would be: _____

_____.

My wedding gown would be: _____

_____.

CHAPTER 5

THE BOYS IN THE BAND

Everyone has a favorite Backstreet Boy. Who's yours? Is it young Nick, the "baby" of the group? Or is it Kevin, with his handsome, movie-star good looks? Maybe it's A. J., the rebel, with his tattoos and 'tude. Or sweet Howie D., the hopeless romantic of the guys. Or is it Brian, last to join the Boys, but first in the hearts of thousands of fans?

Check out the facts on this fab fivesome . . . and pick your die-hard fave!

Brian Littrell

Full name: Brian Thomas Littrell
Nicknames: B-rok, Mr. Joker, Seaver, Frick

Birth date: February 20, 1975

Astrological sign: Pisces

Birthplace: Lexington, Kentucky

Parents: Jackie and Harold

Siblings: Big brother Harold, Jr.

Marital status: Newly wed (September 2000) to Leighanne Wallace

Height: 5'7"

Eyes: Bright blue

Hair: Sandy, somewhere between blond and red

Pets: Chihuahua named Lil Tyk Thomas, a newer dog named Little Leigh, a cat named Missy

Hobbies: Singing, dancing, basketball, and golf

Favorite color: Midnight blue

Favorite food: Macaroni and cheese

Favorite movie: *Star Wars*

Favorite Groups: Boyz II Men, Bobby Brown

Favorite Stars: Tom Hanks, Sandra Bullock

Proudest moment: Brian returned to his high school in Kentucky to direct 45 local choral students in singing background vocals for the song "Perfect Fan." "I always wanted to give back to the school," Brian told a Kentucky newspaper.

Howie Dorough

Full name: Howard Dwaine Dorough
Nicknames: Howie D., Sweet D., Latin Lover
Birth date: August 22, 1973
Astrological sign: Leo
Birthplace: Orlando, Florida
Parents: Paula and Hoke
Siblings: John, Pollyana, Caroline, and Angie. Caroline passed away in 1998.
Marital status: Single
Height: 5'6"
Eyes: Brown
Hair: Brown
Pets: Christopher the cat, Oscar the dog
Hobbies: Weight lifting, waterskiing, dancing, racquetball, and going to the movies
Favorite color: Purple
Favorite food: Asian
Favorite movie: *The Outsiders*
Favorite groups: Jon Secada, Bobby Brown
Favorite star: Tom Hanks
Weirdest talent: Singing Christmas carols in Hawaiian
Most embarrassing moment: When Howie fell off the stage while trying to hype A. J. with his rap during the song "Get Down!"

A. J. McLean

Full name: Alexander James McLean
Nicknames: A. J., Bone
Birth date: January 9, 1978
Astrological sign: Capricorn
Birthplace: West Palm Beach, Florida
Parents: Denise and Bob (A. J.'s parents divorced in 1982).
Marital status: Single, but maybe not for long
Height: 5'9"
Eyes: Brown
Hair: Hmmm . . . sometimes brown, sometimes pink, sometimes blue!
Pets: Three dogs — two black-and-white Shih Tzus named Panda and Bear and a dachshund named Tobi Wan Kenobi
Hobbies: Dancing, basketball, golf, bowling, writing poetry, shopping, and shooting pool
Favorite color: Yellow
Favorite food: Chili cheese fries
Favorite movie: *Pulp Fiction*
Favorite stars: Jennifer Love Hewitt, Geena Davis
Favorite groups: Stone Temple Pilots, Brian McKnight, Take Six, Mariah Carey
Favorite meal at McDonald's: "The MacLean!" A. J. joked

during a radio interview, referring to the "lite" burger McDonald's once offered. In truth, A. J. likes to order a double-quarter-pounder-with-cheese Value Meal.

Most surprising moment: Once, during a tour in Germany, a fan of A. J.'s gave him two rings worth $15,000! It turns out that the fan had taken the rings from her parents. Naturally, A. J. gave the rings back — but he remembered the incident in an on-line chat as "just plain weird."

Kevin Richardson

Full name: Kevin Scott Richardson
Nicknames: Kev, Boo Boo, Train
Birth date: October 3, 1972
Astrological sign: Libra
Birthplace: Lexington, Kentucky
Parents: Ann and Jerald (Kevin's father died in 1991.)
Siblings: Brothers Jerald, Jr.; and Tim
Marital status: Engaged to Kristin Willits
Height: 6'1"
Eyes: Green
Hair: Dark brown
Pets: A black cat named Quincy

Hobbies: Flying, playing keyboards, waterskiing, surfing, swimming, basketball, and hockey

Favorite color: Royal blue

Favorite food: Mom's home cooking

Favorite movies: *Top Gun, The Shawshank Redemption*

Favorite groups: Santana, Aerosmith, Ace of Base

Favorite stars: Nicole Kidman, Liv Tyler

Scariest moment: When the plane he was piloting did a "four-point roll" — "where you stop on the side and then stop upside down," Kevin explained in *Teen People* magazine. "Then we did one where we went a long way upside down and I was just hanging there. That's when I started sweating!"

His *true* love: Sleep! "I love to sleep!" he said in an online chat. "I'm just used to being around loudness — sound checks, fans, hotels . . . so that once I get to sleep it's kind of hard to get me up!"

Nick Carter

Full name: Nickolas Gene Carter

Nicknames: Nicky, Chaos, Mr. Hyper Man, Frack, Messy Marvin

Birth date: January 28, 1980

Astrological sign: Aquarius

Birthplace: Jamestown, New York

Parents: Jane and Bob

Siblings: Sisters Bobbie Jean (B. J.) and Leslie and twins Aaron and Angel

Marital status: Single

Height: 6'1"

Weight: 170 pounds

Eyes: Bright blue

Hair: Blond

Pets: Cats Rocky, Sugar, and Bandit; dogs (pugs) Samson, Simba, and Pepper

Hobbies: Boating, fishing, drawing, basketball, and video games

Favorite color: Forest green

Favorite food: Pizza

Favorite movies: *Alien, Braveheart*

Favorite groups: Journey, Nirvana, Jodeci, Boyz II Men

Favorite stars: Sigourney Weaver, Jeff Goldblum

Biggest fear in life: Sharks! "My fear is being in the water and being attacked by them," Nick said in an on-line chat.

Most embarrassing moment: Ripping his pants in concert, Nick told fans in an on-line chat. "We had ducked down, done a move or something. It felt like it ripped, but I was like 'maybe not.' But then I felt this breeze coming up from somewhere and I put my

Hyper-cool always, the Backstreet Boys are here to stay: The fans want it that way!

Nick is the BSB brain behind their comic book series. "[In it] we're all good guys tryin' to save the world."

"I think you can feel something in our voices," Kev confesses of the band's shimmering harmonies, as he stages a cool move.

Offstage, Brian plays golf — sometimes with
A. J. and cousin Kevin.

Like all the BSB, Brian was proud of their five Grammy nominations for *Millennium*.

A portrait of the band: The Backstreet Boys are [l. to r.] A. J., Howie, Kevin, Nick, and Brian.

A. J. confesses he was "the biggest geek" in high school — look at him now!

A. J.'s been with the band for their (so far) eight years together.

Howie used to be an actor, and may head back in that direction some day.

Howie is candid about the BSB vs. 'N Sync thing: "It's a friendly competition. We're cool with each other. They do their thing and we do ours."

Kevin's hobby? He flies his own airplane.

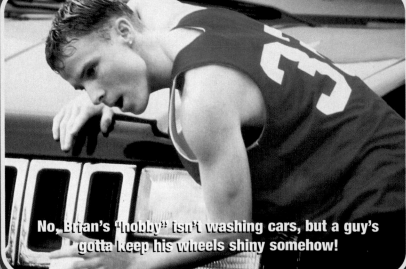

No, Brian's "hobby" isn't washing cars, but a guy's gotta keep his wheels shiny somehow!

"I Want It That Way," their first single off *Millennium*, was their biggest hit ever.

At the *Billboard* Music Awards, the band picked up a trophy — though why Nick showed up with bed-head is anyone's guess!

hand back there and I could actually touch my whole butt!"

How about YOU? Fill in *your* stats and see how you match up to the Boys!

Full name: _____

Nicknames: _____

Birth date: _____

Astrological sign: _____

Birthplace: _____

Parents: _____

Siblings: _____

Height: _____

Weight: _____

Eyes: _____

Hair: _____

Pets: _____

Hobbies: _____

Favorite color: _____

Favorite food: _____

Favorite movie: _____

Favorite groups: _____

Favorite stars: _____

Biggest fear: _____

Most embarrassing moment: _____

Proudest moment: _____

CHAPTER 6

WHAT THE BOYS SAY . . .

Here are the guys' responses to some excellent fan questions. See if you can predict what your favorite Boy will say! Then answer the questions yourself and see how your answers match up with your favorite Boy's answers.

Q. If you weren't a singer, what would you be?
A. J.: "A drama teacher."
Brian: "A schoolteacher."
Howie: "An actor."
Kevin: "In music, maybe playing keys for a rock band."
Nick: "A college student playing basketball."

What do you want to be? _____

Q. What's the most outrageous thing you've ever done?

A. J.: "I flew on a trapeze."

Brian: "Had heart surgery."

Howie: "Bungee jumping."

Kevin: "Climbing into an F16."

Nick: "My whole life's been pretty outrageous!"

What's the most outrageous thing *you've* ever done?

_____

Q. What are your favorite things?

A. J.: "My new house, which I decorated myself. And my car."

Brian: "My health, my family, sports, and my soon-to-be spouse."

Howie: "Spending time with my family, being on the road, trying new food, new nightclubs. Cattle herding in Arizona!"

Kevin: "Traveling, now that we're able to spend more than just eight hours in any city. When I'm in L.A., I go snow boarding [nearby], and out in nature. And my fiancée."

Nick: "Video games and basketball."

What are some of your favorite things?_____

_____

Q. What is your ultimate dream?
A. J.: "I want to be a teacher or do theater, preferably at New York University. Be involved as a head of an organization with multiple charities, like what U2 and REM are doing."
Brian: "To someday become a dad, running around and chasing my kids, changing diapers. And playing golf."
Howie: "To just be able to go out one day and rent an island and party with my family and friends. I also want to meet the Pope."
Kevin: "Operate my own record label."
Nick: "I would like to play basketball in college or in a league overseas. I want to learn martial arts and sail around the world."

What is your ultimate dream? _____

_____

CHAPTER 7

●

SPOTLIGHT ON AARON CARTER

Lest you think Nick Carter is the *only* talented kid in his family, check out lil' bro Aaron. He's currently riding the charts with a new album on the Jive Records label (which came out June 20, 2000) and hitting the tour circuit with his brand-new Aaron Carter 2000 tour!

True, if it weren't for big brother Nick, "I wouldn't be here," Aaron told *Top of the Pops* magazine last year. After Nick's career with the Backstreet Boys took off, Aaron began opening for the Boys in 1997. But Aaron's career was launched at one extra-special concert — in March 1997 in Berlin, Germany. Aaron gave such an awesome performance that night, he was offered a recording contract with Edel Record Company right after the show! The following fall, Aaron released his first single, "Crush On You," followed by "Crazy Little Party Girl," "I'm Gonna Miss You Forever," and "Shake It." By June of 1998 he had an album out — *Aaron Carter.* It went gold in Spain, Norway, Canada, Denmark, and Germany. Since then his songs have grown more and more popular in the United States — especially after the release of "(Have Some) Fun With the Funk" on the *Pokémon: The First Movie* sound track.

Born in Tampa, Florida, moments after his twin sister, Angel, Aaron was a musical kid from the very beginning. In fact, he was in a band called Dead End at age seven! They broke up when Aaron and the other boys couldn't agree on the type of music their band should play. The band was into alternative while Aaron wanted pop.

Aaron and his twin, Angel, are very close. Though she's not a singer and doesn't perform with Aaron, Angel does share her sibling's love of the spotlight. She likes to model — and recently she modeled fashions for a charity show where Aaron was performing. Older sister Leslie, on the other hand, seems to be following in her brothers' footsteps. Thirteen-year-old Leslie Carter recently signed a recording deal with Dreamworks Records.

These days, Aaron is gearing up for his new tour,

practicing dance moves and rehearsing songs. His latest single, "Girl, You Shine," is generating lots of interest and will definitely be included in his new show. When he's not working, this busy twelve-year-old is home-schooled, likes to ride motorcycles, to fish, and to play Nintendo — big surprise, seeing as he's Nick's brother!

Here's a rundown of the need-to-know info on Aaron Carter:

Full name: Aaron Charles Carter (named after his grandfather)
Nicknames: AC and Chuckie
Birth date: December 7, 1987
Birthplace: Tampa, Florida
Family: Parents Robert and Jane. Older sisters B. J. and Leslie, older brother, Nick, and twin sister, Angel
Favorite food: Pizza
Favorite color: Blue
Favorite sports: Basketball, baseball, and swimming
Favorite actor: Sylvester Stallone

CHAPTER 8

●

BETCHA DIDN'T KNOW . . .

Think you know everything there is to know about the Backstreet Boys? Well, maybe you do! But for the few of us who still have a bit more to learn, here are some Backstreet betchas — as in betcha didn't know . . .

Betcha didn't know . . . that Kevin takes an envelope filled with pictures of his family with him on the road when he's touring.

Betcha didn't know . . . that A. J. doesn't drive! Because of his grueling schedule, he's never had time to study for the written part of the driver's exam, so he doesn't have a driver's license yet.

Betcha didn't know . . . that Nick is a licensed scuba diver.

Betcha didn't know . . . that when they started out, Nick and Brian usually shared a hotel room while on the road. Now that things are going well for the boys, they each have their own room.

Betcha didn't know . . . that Brian spent much of his free time this year in Nashville, recording and producing his brother Harold's upcoming country-and-western album.

Betcha didn't know . . . that Nick's new house in the Santa Yhez Valley in California has a small lake, a pool, a barn, and tennis courts.

Betcha didn't know . . . that Howie cracks up when he remembers meeting A. J. for the first time at a talent show in Florida. Because they both wanted to be actors and had a similar look, they were often up for the same parts. "A. J. did this little puppeteering thing to 'Opposites Attract' by Paula Abdul," Howie told *Rolling Stone* magazine. "All I could remember was him having this jeans shirt, these pants and a tie, and a little brief-case!"

Betcha didn't know . . . that in the group's early days Howie used to wear big, baggy M. C. Hammer pants! He loved M. C. Hammer and memorized Hammer's songs and moves.

Betcha didn't know . . . that the CORRECT

spelling of Brian's Chihuahua's name is Lil Tyk Thomas, and that he recently got himself another Chihuahua puppy named Little Leigh.

Betcha didn't know . . . that the Backstreet Boys were the first group ever to perform twice in one Grammy Awards show. Last February at the 42nd Annual Grammy Awards Show, they appeared first to sing their nominated hit, "I Want It That Way," and then later they performed with Elton John.

Betcha didn't know . . . that Howie keeps all his awards and platinum records at his parents' house, which he says looks like a Backstreet museum.

Betcha didn't know . . . that when the Boys were working on their newest CD, they locked themselves in a house with a studio and just kicked back, chillin' and creatin'! A. J. told on-line fans that the guys wanted to create the best possible album. "We were going to try something different this time," he said, "which was to go to the Bahamas to a remote studio inside a house and live there for about two, two-and-a-half weeks with JUST us."

Betcha didn't know . . . that after the 2000 Grammy Awards, the Backstreet Boys hosted a huge, blowout bash — even though they didn't win any awards.

Betcha didn't know . . . that Howie claims he's "never blown his nose" (*Teen* magazine). "I can't do it. I can stand to see blood and puke, but when it comes to anything mucus-oriented, or phlegm, or someone spitting — I gag."

Betcha didn't know . . . that A. J.'s mother says he has a cute way of twirling his clothing between his thumb and forefinger when he's nervous!

Betcha didn't know . . . that back in March 2000, when the Boys let their fans vote on which single from their *Millennium* album they would like released next, "Don't Want You Back" was leading the whole time — until Nick told *TRL*'s Carson Daly that his favorite was "The One." The next day, "The One" jumped into the lead and won the vote!

Betcha didn't know . . . that A. J. has fourteen tattoos, including his two newest tattoos — a sun on the top of his right shoulder and a symbol he created especially for his Johnny No-Name character (the stage name he uses for solo charity performances) on his right shoulder. The funny thing is that with all his tattoos, A. J. is scared to death of getting a shot at the doctor's office!

Betcha didn't know . . . that Nick was in the movie *Edward Scissorhands*! "It would be going too far to say I was actually *in Edward Scissorhands,*" Nick confessed on-line. "Because I was so far in the background that you can't tell it's me!" Nick explained that he is one of the kids playing on a Slip and Slide in the driveway across the street when Edward looks out his window into the neighborhood.

Betcha didn't know . . . that A. J.'s significant other sometimes logs onto BSB chat rooms using A. J.'s screen name and talks to his fans and answers their questions!

CHAPTER 9

THE BSB TRIVIA CHALLENGE

Now that you've had a super-charged Backstreet fact attack, it's time to put your BSB knowledge to the test. If you can correctly answer eight of the following sixteen questions, you qualify as the *perfect* BSB fan.

1. How many Grammy awards did the Backstreet Boys win in February 2000?

Your answer: _____

2. What is the name of the Backstreet Boys' recording label?

Your answer: _____

3. What Elton John song did the Backstreet Boys sing live at the Grammy Awards with Sir Elton himself?

Your answer: _____

4. Which Disney character did Kevin *never* dress up as when he worked at Disney World?

Your answer: _____

5. Who is Tommy Smith?

Your answer: _____

6. What color is Howie's Corvette Stingray?

Your answer: _____

7. What part of Kevin's body does he compare with that of Groucho Marx?

Your answer: _____

8. When the Backstreet Boys were just starting up, they used to hold meetings with their former manager, Lou Pearlman, at what famous restaurant?

Your answer: _____

9. Which member of 'N Sync asked Howie why *he* was never asked to join the Backstreet Boys?

Your answer: _____

10. Which Backstreet Boy landed a role in the movie *Bloom* that's supposed to star Jeff Goldblum?

Your answer: _____

11. When A. J. embarked on a mini-tour as Johnny No Name, for what charity was he playing?

Your answer: _____

12. What is the name of the Backstreet Boys' favorite choreographer?

Your answer: _____

13. Name a band that the Backstreet Boys opened for when they were just starting out.

Your answer: _____

14. What is the name of the sitcom pilot Howie wrote the music for and guest-starred in with Sherman Helmsley?

Your answer: _____

15. In the song "Show Me the Meaning of Being Lonely," what line comes before "to an endless love/There's no control/Are you with me now?"

Your answer: _____

16. Which Backstreet Boy guest-starred as a mysterious young man on the May 15, 2000, season finale of *Roswell*?

Your answer: _____

Check out the answers below to see how you scored. Are you a Backstreet Brainiac, or is it back to Backstreet basics for you?

1. none
2. Jive Records
3. "Philadelphia Freedom"
4. Tigger

5. the BSB's keyboardist
6. purple
7. his eyebrows
8. TGI Friday's
9. Chris Kirkpatrick
10. Howie
11. VH1 Save the Music
12. Fatima
13. REO Speedwagon, Kenny G, Boyz II Men
14. *Love Thy Neighbor*
15. "If only guilty roads"
16. Howie Dorough

CHAPTER 10

●

BEHIND THE HITS

What's your favorite BSB tune? Is it the soulful 'n' sweet "I Want It That Way" or the old-time fave "Everybody (Backstreet's Back)"? Or maybe you're a huge fan of "Show Me the Meaning of Being Lonely" or "Larger Than Life" or "The One."

Everyone has a favorite BSB song — even the Boys themselves! Check out the facts on all your favorite BSB hits . . . then use the funky Millennium-ometer to see how they rate!

THE MILLENNIUM–OMETER!

1   Sorry, Guys, But Ewww!
2   Not the Boys' Best, for Sure

47

The Tunes

"Don't Want You Back"

Okay, so you're thinking, What's up with this song, guys? True, it's a rockin' tune, but *hello*?! It's about *breaking up*! Kevin explains that the song wasn't meant to be a downer. It was just meant to express the true feelings of all five Boys — about how they never know WHY people show an interest in them. All five Boys have said that in show biz it's hard to know who your real friends are.

Here's what Kevin had to say about why the Boys cut this track: "There's a genuine fear deep down in all of us," he told *Teen People,* "of why someone's talking to you, and why someone's interested in you. Is it because you're Kevin or Brian, or is it because you're in a group called the Backstreet Boys? And not just in dating, but in friendships and in business, too."

Still, even though some fans call it "the breakup song," Kevin says it's one of his faves — but not his absolute favorite.

A. J. thinks this song is one of their best, too. He thinks most boy BSB fans tend to rate this song higher than girl BSB fans.

What do you think?
I give this song a _____ on the Millennium-ometer.

"Show Me the Meaning of Being Lonely"

Of all the BSB songs, this is the one all five hold closest to their hearts. "I personally have strong feelings for [that song]," Nick told *Teen People*. Though the song was written before the passing of one of the Boys' favorite producers, Denniz Pop, the lyrics really hit home for Nick and the others every time they sing it. In fact, Nick even remembers recording the song in Sweden and how he felt Denniz's presence as they sang.

Brian has strong feelings for this song, too. In the video for SMTMOBL, Brian watches himself in a hospital bed. Filming this part of the video was Brian's idea. He believes it best expresses how he felt when he was in the hospital for heart surgery.

This song was an emotional ride for Howie, too. The words remind him of how he felt when his sister died a couple of years ago from a disease called lupus. Howie admits this is one of his favorite songs on the album.

What do you think?
I give this song a _____ on the Millennium-ometer!

"Larger Than Life"

A. J. has told reporters time and time again that he really hopes BSB fans understand what this song is about. At first, it may sound as if the BSB have humongous egos and think they're "larger than life." But that's not what they're saying at all. In fact, the guys intended this slammin' tune as a thank-you to all their fans around the world. What they're saying is that their *fans* (yes, *you*!) are larger than life! "Every time we're down/You can make it right/And that makes you larger than life." A. J. says hands down that this is his favorite BSB song.

What do you think?
I give this song a _____ on the Millennium-ometer!

"The One"

This is the awesome song that won the vote when the Boys decided to let their *fans* be the ones to pick their next single release! Traditionally, band members, record producers, agents, and managers sit down and decide *what's* going to be released *when*. But the Boys had the terrific idea of letting their fans decide what their next single would be. With a little help from MTV and from radio stations across the country, the Boys held a contest. Fans called in or voted on-line for which song they preferred: "The One," "Don't Want You Back," and "It's Gotta Be You." Thousands of fans voted (300,000 fans to be exact!), and every day for as long as the contest went on each song took a turn at being in the lead! Then Nick made an appearance on MTV's *Total Request Live* and happened to mention he liked "The One" best.

Well, that was that! "The One" took off like a rocket — nearly doubling its amount of votes in one day and becoming the next single released.

What do you think?

I give this song a _____ on the Millennium-ometer!

"Don't Want to Lose You Now"

So which song *is* Kevin's favorite? A short while back, Kevin told a Rhode Island radio DJ that "Don't Want to Lose You Now" was his fave. In fact, during the contest, he said, "I'm kind of hoping they'll pick 'Don't Want to Lose You Now' just because that's one of my favorite songs . . . it always has been, ever since we recorded it."

What do you think?

I give this song a _____ on the Millennium-ometer!

"The Perfect Fan"

By now everybody knows that this sweet song was written by Brian for his mother. (Aw!) After he wrote it, Brian went to Kentucky to record it with his high school choir — something that they, for sure, will never forget! The song has since become a tribute to *all* the Boys' moms — and it even makes their fans' moms cry when they sing it in concert!

What do you think?

I give this song a _____ on the Millennium-ometer!

"Spanish Eyes"

This is Howie's *other* favorite song because of its distinctive Latin flavor. (He admits it's a toss-up between "Spanish Eyes" and "Show Me the Meaning of Being Lonely.") Howie has always enjoyed Latin music. He's even said that he'd like to work with such Latin music greats as Carlos Santana and Gloria Estefan.

What do you think?

I give this song a _____ on the Millennium-ometer!

"Back to Your Heart"

Kevin told a reporter from *CDNOW* that this song — which he wrote himself — is very personal. "It's about a guy who thinks the grass is greener on the other side but finds out that it's not. About a guy who finally realizes what he has. It can be about a lot of things — the business, a relationship, a love life. You need to find a balance."

What do you think?

I give this song a _____ on the Millennium-ometer!

My favorite Backstreet Boys CD is _____.

My favorite Backstreet Boys song is _____.

My favorite Backstreet Boys music video is _____

_____.

CHAPTER 11

WE'RE ALL CONNECTED

AND YOU COULD BE CONNECTED TO THE BOYS!

They say everyone in the world is connected to everyone else through six other people. Know what that means? It means that there are just six people separating you from the Backstreet Boy of your dreams!

Okay, check it out. . . .

Let's say you wanted to connect two famous people who travel in different circles. First, check out who they've starred with in a movie or TV show and connect them that way. Or, find out who they share a birthday or birthplace with and connect them like that.

Here's how each of the Boys connects to a popular celeb:

A. J. McLean to **Sarah Michelle Gellar.**

A. J. connects to . . .

Elton John. They sang together at the Grammys. Elton John connects to . . .

Jonathan Taylor Thomas. Elton wrote the music for *The Lion King* and JTT was the voice of Simba. JTT connects to . . .

Jason Priestley. They starred together in the TV movie *Common Ground*. Jason connects to . . .

Tori Spelling. She was his co-star on *Beverly Hills, 90210*. Tori connects to . . .

David Boreanaz. He and Tori share the same birthday: May 16. And David starred in *Buffy the Vampire Slayer* with . . .

Sarah Michelle Gellar!

Now let's connect **Nick Carter** with **Jennifer Aniston.**

Nick Carter connects to . . .

Johnny Depp. Nick had a teeny part in *Edward Scissorhands* with Johnny Depp. Johnny connects to . . .

Leonardo DiCaprio. They starred together in the film *What's Eating Gilbert Grape?* Leo connects to . . .

Demi Moore. They share the same birthday, November 11. Demi connects to . . .

Bruce Willis. They used to be married. Bruce connects to . . .

Matthew Perry. They both starred in the movie *The Whole Nine Yards,* and Matthew stars in the TV show *Friends* with . . .

Jennifer Aniston!

Now let's connect **Howie Dorough** and **Julia Roberts**.

Howie Dorough had a small part in the movie *Parenthood,* which starred . . .

Steve Martin. Steve was born in Waco, Texas, and so was . . .

Jennifer Love Hewitt, who starred in the TV show *Party of Five* with . . .

Neve Campbell. Neve starred in the first *Scream* movie, which also featured . . .

Drew Barrymore. Drew stars in the movie *Charlie's Angels* with . . .

Cameron Diaz, who starred in the movie *My Best Friend's Wedding* with none other than . . .

Julia Roberts!

And here's how **Kevin Richardson** connects to actress **Gwyneth Paltrow**.

Kevin connects to . . .

Kristin Willits, his fiancee. Kristin toured as a dancer for . . .

Cher, who starred in the movie *Mermaids* with . . .

Winona Ryder. Winona used to date . . .

Matt Damon, who is best friends with . . .

Ben Affleck. And Ben used to date . . .

Gwyneth Paltrow!

And last but not least, here's how **Brian Littrell** connects to his wife, **Leighanne Wallace!**

Brian is in the Backstreet Boys with his cousin . . .

Kevin Richardson. Both Boys appeared in a TV documentary with . . .

Shania Twain. Shania shares a birthday (August 28) with . . .

Jason Priestley, who starred in the movie *Dill Scallion* AND has the same birthday (August 28) as country-and-western singer . . .

LeAnn Rimes. LeAnn also starred in *Dill Scallion* with actor/singer . . .

Travis Tritt, who asked this fellow Marietta, Georgia, native to be in his first music video — yes, it was none other than . . .

Leighanne Wallace!

See? That's how people from different walks of life connect. You can connect people through birthdays, birthplaces, the schools they attended — whatever! So give it a go and see which BSB (one, or all five!) *you* connect with!

_____

(you)

_____

(your first connection and how you made it)

_____

(your second connection and how you made it)

_____

(your third connection and how you made it)

_____

(your fourth connection and how you made it)

_____

(your fifth connection and how you made it)

_____

(the Backstreet Boy of your dreams!)

CHAPTER 12

●

PICTURE YOURSELF IN THE FRONT ROW!

Were you able to get tickets to the Backstreet Boys' Into the Millennium tour before it sold out (in 73 minutes!)?

The lucky ones who managed to snag tickets to the concert already know how incredible it was. But the rest of us, well, we could only dream about being there live (sigh!) and start saving for this fall (2000), when we'll get another chance at seeing them live in concert!

In the meantime, just kick back and check out the inside scoop on what the Into the Millennium tour was like. And remember: At least in your daydreams, it'll be YOU in the front row, and YOU the Boys pick to join them onstage for a serenade!

You and the Backstreet Boys LIVE!

As most Backstreet Boys fans know, the BSB concert experience doesn't begin at the arena or stadium. Instead, it begins at the hotel you've managed to learn is the one the Boys are staying at while in town!

It's true — before every concert the word begins to spread. Maybe it starts with an innocent whisper from a bellboy to a front desk clerk, "You know, I just delivered a pizza to Nick Carter's room." And all at once, the wheels are in motion: The desk clerk calls her friend, who calls her sister, who tells all her friends, and WHAM! The next thing you know there are a hundred screaming girls in the hotel lobby!

Even if it's 4:30 A.M. and the concert isn't for another fifteen hours — as soon as word slips out that the infamous black buses with their gold swirls have pulled into the hotel parking lot, it's a free-for-all.

So somehow you've managed to find out that the Backstreet Boys are in town at a hotel near your house. The next step is begging your parents to get out of bed and drive you there! You spend the next fifteen minutes fixing your hair and picking out the perfect outfit (something Nick will surely notice!), then, without breakfast, you're in the car and headed to the hotel.

When you get to the hotel, your heart nearly stops beating when you see the Boys' buses in the parking lot! There are ten tour buses and fourteen tractor trailer trucks in the entourage! Ignoring the fact that there are already lots of other girls there, you race up to the bus and try to guess who's inside. Was that A. J., you wonder, or Howie? It's hard to tell because the bus windows are dark.

Around you, everybody is screaming at the top of their lungs. Some carry flowers, some have signs, and others wear Backstreet Boys tattoos painted on their faces. You have a flower and a tattoo, too, and a camera, because you're determined to get a picture of you and your favorite Boy.

There's a rumor going around that the Boys are heading off to a press conference at the place where the concert will be held. Should you go? There's another rumor that Brian is heading out to play a round of golf. Should you go there instead? Just as you're trying to make the agonizing decision, the bus doors open — and Nick steps out!

The screaming grows louder, and you're sure you're shouting louder than anyone! "Nick! I love you! Can I have an autograph!" If only he'd look in your direction!

Nick begins signing autographs, but you're not close enough. You squeeze through the crowd, pulling your mother behind you. Before you know it, you're just a few feet away from Nick! You hold up your cam-

TIPS FROM THE EXPERTS ON KEEPING TABS ON THE BOYS

These tips were compiled by fans who follow the Boys' every move. *(Saint Petersburg Times)*

Be Cool
If you spot a BSB, don't pounce. Your fave cutie will *not* want to talk to you if you scream and run at him.

era at just the right second, because he sees it and flashes you a smile! "Would you like to get a picture of us together?" Nick asks.

You can barely answer. Before you can nod, Nick's putting his arm around you and smiling. Luckily, your Mom isn't gaga, and she takes the camera from you and snaps a picture. The very picture you know you're going to rush to develop and probably carry around with you for the rest of your life!

Nick kisses your cheek (OMG!) and disappears into the hotel. It all happened so fast! You feel like laughing and crying at the same time. But the best is yet to come — your Backstreet Boys live experience is just beginning!

Next, it's off to the concert!

You do a spot-check with your friends before leaving the house at noon. So what if the concert still isn't for seven hours???

You have everything you'll need: your NICK ROCKS! poster, a Beanie Baby dressed in a wedding dress (that's for Brian, Kevin, and A. J. who are getting married), a pack of green glow sticks to activate in the dark, pocket money (for a T-shirt, a BSB comic, and a program), and your camera.

You're ready. You hang out in the parking lot for the next million hours, talking to other fans and sharing stories of Backstreet Boys sightings. You tell your story about meeting Nick at the hotel a hundred times. Your mother verifies the story, and you become a minor celebrity!

Finally, it's time to go in. Inside the arena, the sound is deafening! Everyone is yelling and screaming. You make your way to your seats . . . in the front row! You stare at the stage and let it all soak in. The stage is shaped like a pentagon, right smack in the middle of the arena. There are five video screens high above, one for each Boy. Your heart

Be Careful
If you go on-line and chat with other fans to get the scoop—be careful. Sometimes people like to go on-line and pretend they're BSB. Keep in mind, the real BSB have a very busy schedule and can't spend as much time as they'd like in chat rooms with their fans. Chances are if someone has tons of time to e-mail you every single day, he's not the real deal.

has not stopped thumping since — well, since you saw Nick that morning!

Finally, the lights go out. It's concert time! Instantly, thousands of glow sticks are activated, and a green fluorescent glow covers the arena. The stage magically lights up in an icy blue color, the same blue color as their *Millennium* CD cover. Above the screams, the music begins: It's the theme from *Star Wars*! Then, all at once, the five Boys you love are entering the arena — from the ceiling!

They emerge in a puff of smoke from a box high at one end of the stage, then are lowered from the ceiling while riding on glowing surfboards and boogie boards! They're dressed in dark armor suits (Nick looks adorable!) and space-age cargo pants. They start "surfing" right over your head just as the *Star Wars* theme stops and the music from "Larger Than Life" begins. You can't believe you're in the same room with the Backstreet Boys!

Nick takes the microphone first. You're waving at him like crazy! "Remember me?" you're shouting. "I love you, Nick!" Nick points to his new, short haircut that's all spiked up. "What do you think?" he asks the audience. Everyone goes nuts.

The Boys sing "The One," and "Quit Playing Games with My Heart," all the while dangling, twisting, turning, and dancing in the air above the crowd! Below them, their ten dancers are moving to the music in perfect choreography. You're dancing in front of your seat with your best friend and your mom — you probably won't sit once during the entire show!

Finally, the Boys come down to earth, then leave for a quick costume change while the band plays on. When they come back out, they're all wearing white! They start singing "Everybody (Backstreet's Back)," and you're screaming like crazy! You can't take your eyes off their moves — they're unbelievable. The Boys go directly into "We Got It Goin' On" and "That's the Way We Like It." You're hoping Nick will notice you, but you can't seem to catch his attention.

During "Back to Your Heart," Kevin looks and sounds amazing, playing a white grand piano and singing all alone onstage. Nick sits in with the band and plays along on the drums. You never knew he could play like that! He's awesome!

During the next song, A. J. makes you laugh when he bounces a basketball onstage to the beat of the music. And Brian surprises you with his violin playing — who knew he was such a talented musician?

But the funniest is when Howie starts doing back flips in the air during "Get Down (You're the One for Me)!" When he's finished, he can barely walk straight!

The whole time, Nick and A. J. are joking around on-stage with the dancers. Then Howie raps, and Nick calls him Funky D.!

After another costume change, the Boys come out in trench coats and sing "As Long As You Love Me." They dance a cool routine as they sing, using steel chairs. After that it's "Don't Want to Lose You Now." They're really rockin' now, and you can't believe what a great time you're having. Your throat is sore from screaming, and your NICK ROCKS! poster is ripping from waving it so much. It couldn't possibly get better. . . .

Then suddenly, there's a woman tapping you on the shoulder. "Would you and your mother like to join the Boys onstage for the next song?" she asks.

"YES!" you scream. "YES! YES! YES!"

Your legs shake as you and your mom follow the woman backstage. On the side of the stage, there are four other girls and their mothers. It's a dream come true!

The music for "The Perfect Fan" begins. This is it! One by one the guys come to take a girl and parade her around the stage. You almost die when you see Nick heading toward you! You can barely breathe!

"Hey, I know you!" he says. "From the hotel." He smiles at you and you totally melt. He sings a verse from "The Perfect Fan," then gives you — and your mother! — a kiss on the cheek!

When you return to your seat, you're in such a fog you almost miss "Don't Want You Back." You watch the Boys dance, but all you can think about is Nick while you touch the place on your cheek where he kissed you.

There is no way you're ever going to wash your cheek again!

Another costume change and the Boys are in three-piece suits and singing "Spanish Eyes." Then "I'll Never Break Your Heart," with one chorus in Spanish. Then "No One Comes Close" — Nick really gets into singing that one.

Another costume change and it's pin-striped suits for "All I Have to Give." Then the boys end the show with your all-time favorite song, "Show Me the Meaning of Being Lonely." It couldn't have been more perfect! As the Boys leave the stage one by one, you don't want it to end. The lights go down and you activate your last green glow stick. The arena is glowing green once again.

Finally, after a *long* two minutes, the Backstreet Boys are back! They sing "It's Gotta Be You," then introduce the band and the dancers and spray confetti all over the crowd!

At that second, you know it's coming — the end of the show! When the first few notes of "I Want It That Way" begin, you're crying for real. The Boys sing a powerful rendition of "That Way," and with a final wave to the crowd, they're gone.

As the lights in the arena come on you fall into your seat, exhausted. You vow to remember every second, every dance step, every cute expression on the Boys' faces. The fireworks, the flames shooting in the air, the beautiful voices . . . they'll all be in your dreams forever.

CHAPTER 13

●

THE BACKSTREET PROJECT

It's never been done before in the history of all-boy bands. But leave it to the Backstreet Boys to make history and become *SUPERHEROES*!

The Boys recently teamed with Spider-Man's creator to create their very own comic book called *Menace of the Death Queen*. But before all the credit is given to comics master Stan Lee, let it be known that this project came about thanks to the awesome creative talents of Backstreet Boy Nick Carter. Nick, an avid fan of drawing and cartooning, always dreamed of creating his own comic book. So when he sent Stan Lee his story ideas and Stan Lee agreed to work with him to create a Backstreet Boys comic, Nick was stoked!

"It was a collaboration," Stan Lee told *Entertainment Weekly*. "We were in constant touch, and when the prototype came out, the boys went over it again and made little changes here and there so the dialogue would sound exactly the way they speak."

Nick is especially excited about the whole thing. "Each of the characters is great and shows a side of us that we would like to be or already are," he told *USA Today*.

Stan Lee reveals the plot on Backstreetproject.com: The Backstreet Boys are in the middle of doing a sold-out stadium concert when a spaceship crash-lands next to the stadium.

Lee explains that the young singers rescue a beautiful alien creature from the ship. The Boys learn she is a visitor to Earth, here on a mission to protect our planet from an alien invasion. The beautiful alien gives each of the Boys a magical amulet. When the Boys wear their amulets, they have supernatural powers.

Nick

Nick's amulet gives him ancient Ninja powers and transforms him into a master martial artist. Nick's alter ego carries a sharp sword and can defeat the fiercest enemies in the blink of an eye.

Brian

Brian's amulet allows him to jump to impossible new heights. Brian's comic counterpart can also generate a mystic ball of energy that looks like a basketball.

A. J.

A. J.'s amulet gives him the power to accurately hit a target with any weapon — even with laser blasters.

Kevin

Kevin's charm makes him as strong as a champion weight lifter.

Howie

Howie's superpower is a little more mind-blowing. He becomes telepathic! He can project stunning three-dimensional images of anything from pizza to race cars.

*   *   *

As Nick told *USA Today,* "Basically, we're all good guys trying to save the world."

So where can you get a copy of *Menace of the Death Queen*? This 32-page, full-color limited-edition comic book is sold exclusively on-line at Backstreetproject.com and at Backstreet Boys concerts.

CHAPTER 14

●

WINNERS IN OUR HEARTS

When the announcement was made in February 2000 that the Backstreet Boys had been nominated for five Grammy awards, BSB fans all over the world cheered and celebrated like crazy. *Finally!* The Boys were going to receive the recognition they so rightly deserved! Having been passed over by the American Music Awards just a few months before and by the 1999 Grammys, the Boys were thrilled by their five nominations and were hopeful they'd take home at least one of the small golden statues.

And the nominations were:

Record of the Year for "I Want It That Way"

Album of the Year for *Millennium*

Best Pop Album for *Millennium*

Song of the Year (Songwriters Award) for "I Want It That Way"

Best Pop Performance by a Duo or Group with Vocals for "I Want It That Way"

On the night of the Grammy Awards in February 2000, the Boys arrived early at the Staples Center in Los Angeles for the dress rehearsal. In addition to being psyched about their nominations, they were also totally revved up for the night of performances that lay ahead — the most exciting part being their own performance with superstar musician Elton John!

Actually, the Boys had worked with their good friend Sir Elton several times before but, as Brian said in a radio interview, none of those projects was ever televised.

Elton John wanted the boys to join him in singing one of his famous songs, "Philadelphia Freedom." That was great news for Nick, Brian, Howie, and Kevin, who were all fans of the popular song from the seventies. But the funny thing was, A. J. had never heard "Philadelphia Freedom" before! The first time he heard it was two days before they performed it at the Grammys!

"All the guys were telling me, 'Oh, A. J., once you hear it, you'll know it. I'm sure you've heard it!'" A. J.

told a radio interviewer. But as it turned out, A. J. really *hadn't* heard the song before.

A. J. did manage to learn "Philadelphia Freedom" in the following two days and everything turned out just fine. In fact, during the final rehearsal the day of the Grammys, Elton paid a visit to the Boys' dressing room to hang out and practice the song. He also helped them work out some background vocals for the tune. They all exchanged ideas about how they were going to perform.

The Boys are big Elton fans, but Elton John proved to be a huge BSB fan, too! Grammy.com reported that during the Grammys rehearsal, Elton playfully plunked out the notes to "I Want It That Way" on his piano until the Boys joined him onstage and chimed in on the song.

That night, while the Grammys were broadcast live all over the world, the boys waited anxiously to take the stage for their first performance. This one would be on their own — without Elton. When it was their turn to go on (right after Whitney Houston) they walked out onstage singing their nominated hit, "I Want It That Way." Judging by the thunderous applause before, during, and after their performance, the audience was confident the Boys would be leaving the Staples Center with a Grammy award that night.

But, as millions of fans know by now, it was not meant to be. Like their fellow talented pop superstars Britney Spears and Ricky Martin, the Backstreet Boys didn't win any awards that night. But that didn't bring them down.

Despite losing in all their nominated categories, the Boys psyched themselves up for their second big appearance of the evening. After Britney Spears sang, they took the stage and kicked off an awesome performance, paying homage to past musical legends in an a cappella medley. They began with the Bee Gees' "How Deep Is Your Love," then segued into the Temptations' "Papa Was a Rolling Stone," followed by "I'll Make Love to You."

The medley was their own idea, according to Brian's report in a radio interview later that week. "I think we were trying to touch base with decades of music from the past. We wanted to pick different acts and different groups that had really made an impact for a long, long time."

The medley was all part of a grand segue into their hit, "Show Me the Meaning of Being Lonely." It was during that chart-topping tune that Elton John joined them onstage! Elton sang their song with them, then they went right into "Philadelphia Freedom."

"It was pretty breathtaking," Brian confessed in the radio interview. "We stand up onstage all the time and perform, but standing up with [Elton John] was definitely a tribute."

When they were finished, the audience went wild! A. J. later told a radio interviewer that, right after "Philadelphia Freedom," he hugged Elton John goodbye and caught his finger on a sharp gold appliqué on Elton's Versace jacket. Luckily, it wasn't too deep a wound. In fact, A. J. is pretty proud of it! "With this scar on the top of my hand in between my knuckles I will never, ever forget Elton John!"

The Boys will be the first to tell you how cool they are with the whole not-winning-any-Grammys thing. By the time the night was over, the Boys headed to their post-Grammys bash with the memories of a truly unforgettable experience onstage with the legendary Sir Elton. Plus they made Grammy history as the only band ever to perform twice in one Grammy Awards show! "We had a wonderful time," A. J. said in a radio interview a few days after the Grammy Awards. "And I mean even though we didn't take home any awards, I could leave happy with my head high and so could the rest of us because we had a [kickin'] performance."

Kevin agreed, and said that he wasn't surprised the Boys lost to Santana in the Album of the Year category. He even admitted he has a copy of Santana's winning *Supernatural* album and thinks it's great!

"Hey, we lost to Sting and Santana," Kevin said jokingly to a Toronto disc jockey. "Wow! I would lose to them any day!"

And speaking of Sting, the Boys recently had the chance to sing onstage with this legend of rock and roll too! The place was New York City, the date was April 11, 2000, and the reason for the performance was the taping of VH1's "Divas: Men Strike Back." And wouldn't you know it, the Backstreet Boys stole the show again! Impressive, since the "other" musical guests included Enrique Iglesias, Sting, D'Angelo, Tom Jones, Christina Aguilera, and Sisqó!

The show (which aired on April 18, 2000) originally ran for over three hours. What the world finally saw on TV was an edited one-hour version. "Divas: Men Strike Back" was a fun 'n' fab musical showcase for the best — and hunkiest! — male musicians around!

The Boys were more than just a musical smash that night: They made fashion news, too. Kevin went onstage lookin' way cool and very sharp in a dark gray ankle-length skirt over pants! Only Kev could pull off that look! Brian wore his usual all-white and Nick looked cute in a long jacket and maroon shirt. Howie and A. J. impressed the crowd with their basic male-diva black.

First, the Boys were introduced by actress Jenna

Elfman (from the TV show *Dharma and Greg*) and walked onstage singing "The One." As the girls in the audience cheered, the Boys moved on to "Show Me the Meaning of Being Lonely." After some more deafening applause, they ended with "I Want It That Way" — and were joined onstage by Sting! Later in the show, the Boys took the stage with Sting yet again for one of his huge hits, "Don't Stand So Close to Me."

For the grand finale, all of the performers joined together to sing another of Sting's biggest hits, "Every Breath You Take." After the show, critics raved about the Boys' fantastic harmonies during this song (they sang a cappella) and made everyone wonder once again why the Backstreet Boys didn't win any Grammy awards!

All in all, with the unbelievable experiences the Boys have had during the past year — sharing the stage with rock-and-roll legends and selling out concerts across the country — the Boys don't waste a minute dwelling on their Grammy losses. Besides, the Boys have always been winners in the eyes of the fans. A few short months after the Grammys broadcast, BSB won the Nickelodeon Kids Choice Award for Best Musical Group. And the Boys are already looking ahead to the future! To more cool award shows and nominations . . . and more opportunities to meet and perform with other great musicians!

CHAPTER 15

●

BATTLE OF THE BANDS!

YOU Give the Awards!

Will the feuding ever stop?

Well, according to the guys, the "feud" between BSB and 'N Sync, which, according to the media, has been going on for years, *never* really existed at all!

True, when the Boys' record label, Jive Records, recently signed 'N Sync, the Boys weren't too keen on the idea. At first, it seemed like a conflict of interest. But they've come to accept it, realizing that as long as everyone's working hard to put out good music, everything will work out.

"They have their sound and we have ours," Howie

said in an on-line interview. And Joey Fatone, one of the members of 'N Sync, agrees. "They're five guys and we're five guys!" Joey joked in the *Philippine Star.* "That's the similarity! I guess people can tell at this point which music is 'N Sync and which music is Backstreet Boys."

"We don't have anything against those guys personally at all," Kevin told a Houston interviewer. "We think they're good guys. We think they're good singers."

"They're trying to pursue their dreams like we're trying to pursue ours," Kevin added.

Joey Fatone of 'N Sync agrees with Kevin that the whole "rivalry" thing was just a rumor. "The competition is nonexistent," he told the *Philippine Star.* "It's only the press sometimes, which makes it look bigger than it really is."

Joey adds that they've known the Backstreet Boys for some time. Chris Kirkpatrick of 'N Sync and Howie Dorough know each other because they studied in the same school and were members of the same choir back in high school. "We say hi to each other, but because of our busy schedules we don't get a chance to be the best of friends."

A few months ago, the Boys and 'N Sync battled it out on the pop charts with their successful singles "Show Me the Meaning of Being Lonely" and "Bye, Bye,

Bye." Each song took a turn in the number-one spot on the charts, and as for the videos, both battled for number one consistently on MTV's *Total Request Live*.

But battling and rivalry aside, there is one thing both these terrific groups have in common: their concern for those who are less fortunate. Every member of Backstreet Boys and 'N Sync has contributed to many worthwhile charities. A. J. has Save the Music Foundation; Brian has an Endowment Fund for Pediatric Cardiology. Ever since Howie's sister died from lupus two years ago, he's been raising tons of money for research for this disease. In addition, they've *all* worked to raise money for tornado victims, the Make a Wish Foundation, the Columbine College Fund, and many others.

But one recent charity project has sparked lots of interest because it has the guys from BSB and the guys from 'N Sync working *together*! The project benefits the Nordoff-Robbins Music Therapy Foundation, which helps disabled and autistic children through music therapy. Both BSB and 'N Sync united with other musicians like the Moffatts and Aaron Carter to form the Bravo All Stars. The Bravo All Stars cut a single called "Let the Music Heal Your Soul" and all the profits from its sale will benefit the foundation!

So the next time you hear those nasty rumors

about BSB and 'N Sync and World War III, remember that these guys actually like and respect one another! And if you *still* have doubts, grab a copy of "Let the Music Heal Your Soul" and play it over and over until you see the light!

So, who's YOUR fave — Backstreet Boys or 'N Sync? Vote for your favorites in every category.

Best album:
Millennium   ——
No Strings Attached   ——
Best song:
"Show Me the Meaning of Being Lonely"   ——
"Bye, Bye, Bye"   ——
Best music video:
Show Me the Meaning of Being Lonely   ——
Bye, Bye, Bye   ——
Best choreography:
The Backstreet Boys   ——
'N Sync   ——

Favorite Backstreet Boys song:_____

Favorite 'N Sync song: _____

Favorite Backstreet Boys music video:_____

Favorite 'N Sync music video: _____

Battle of the babes:

(Circle the boy you think is hottest in each band and write his name in the space provided. Then, from the two choices, vote for the Ultimate Musical Hottie!)

Nick Carter

Howie Dorough

Brian Littrell   _____

A. J. McLean   (cutest from BSB)

Kevin Richardson

Lance Bass

J. C. Chasez

Joey Fatone   _____

Chris Kirkpatrick   (cutest from 'N Sync)

Justin Timberlake

Now you're down to two hotties. Who is your choice for Ultimate Musical Hottie? _____

CHAPTER 16

•

BACKSTREET BOYS DISCOGRAPHY

Albums

Backstreet Boys (international release) Jive/Zomba, 1995
Backstreet Boys (American release, additional cuts) 1997
Millennium Jive Records, 1999
BSB 2000 (working title) Jive Records, 2000

Singles

"We've Got It Goin' On"
"Quit Playin' Games with My Heart"

"Everybody (Backstreet's Back)"
"All I Have to Give"
"Backstreet's Back" (international release) Jive/Zomba,
1997

The Songs

Backstreet Boys
"We've Got It Goin' On"
"Quit Playin' Games with My Heart"
"As Long As You Love Me"
"Everybody (Backstreet's Back)"
"All I Have to Give"
"Anywhere for You"
"Hey, Mr. DJ (Keep Playin' This Song)"
"I'll Never Break Your Heart"
"Darlin'"
"Get Down (You're the One for Me)"
"Set Adrift on Memory Bliss"
"If You Want to Be a Good Girl (Get Yourself a Bad Boy)"

Millennium
"Larger Than Life"
"I Want It That Way"
"Show Me the Meaning of Being Lonely"
"It's Gotta Be You"

"I Need You Tonight"
"Don't Want You Back"
"Don't Wanna Lose You Now"
"The One"
"Back to Your Heart"
"Spanish Eyes"
"No One Else Comes Close"
"The Perfect Fan"

Videos

All Access Video
A Night Out with the Backstreet Boys
Homecoming — Live in Orlando

CHAPTER 18

●

INTO THE MILLENNIUM . . . AND BEYOND!

What's up next for the Backstreet Boys? Oh, nothin' much. Except maybe . . .

A NEW ALBUM!

AND A NEW EARTH-SHATTERING CONCERT TOUR!

And about a zillion other things — from solo projects to charity events to filmmaking!

In the next few months you can expect a lot from the Boys. Having caught some much-needed R&R after their Into the Millennium tour, the Boys plan to be in everybody's face as much as they can! Here's a sneak peek at what lies ahead:

- A new CD jam-packed with hits (to be released October 10, 2000)
- A new tour (fall 2000)
- A new wife for Brian in September 2000. Kevin's and A. J.'s wedding dates are hush hush!
- For Howie, a new TV pilot called *Love Thy Neighbor.* Not only will he guest star, he'll write the music for the show, too. He's also appearing in a new film currently called *Bloom* with Jeff Goldblum. Howie told a fan on-line: "I'm actually playing a bully, believe it or not, something totally opposite of me. It's going to be a good acting stretch for me, so we will see what happens with it."
- A. J. will hit the road — *solo!* He's touring with the BSB's back-up band as Johnny No-Name (or Johnny Suede). And it's all for charity. The tour benefits the Save the Music Foundation — a charity that helps schools raise money for music programs. A. J.'s mom, Denise, told MTV that he'll sing covers of Eminem, Stone Temple Pilots, Brian McKnight, plus his own song, "If You Knew What I Know."
- Also for A. J., he's got his ten-year high school reunion coming up, which he is extremely excited about! "I cannot wait to go to my ten-year re-

union," he told *USA Today,* "because I was looked on as the biggest geek!"

- For all the Boys, a solo album project with members of Backstreet Boys AND members of 'N Sync!
- A few months ago the Boys launched their first "Webisodes" on the Internet — animated stories based on their comic characters from the Backstreet Project. There will be new Webisodes every few months!

What do YOU think about the Backstreet Boys latest CD?

My favorite new song is: _____

My favorite new music video is: _____

My favorite Backstreet Boy is: _____

So NOW answer the question: Where will you be this October 7 . . . and every October 7 from now on?

Hopefully, you answered: "Out celebrating the Official Backstreet Boys Day in true BSB style with my best buds!"

Now that you've satisfied your craving for the stats on your favorite five fellas and clued into where they've been and what they've been up to, you're one step closer to becoming "The Perfect BSB Fan!" So start socking away some of that allowance each week and make sure you're ready when tix for their next tour go on sale. You'll want to be there in the front row with your sign and your glow stick and your teddy bears, to show the Boys just how dedicated you are!

And if you don't get to see 'em live this time around — don't fret. You'll have plenty more chances. The Boys took on the U.S. at the start of the millennium . . . and the way things are going for Nick, Brian, A. J., Howie, and Kevin — they'll be around for a long time . . . *into the millennium!*